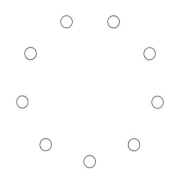

The Fasting Practice

A Four-Session Guide to Offering Your Whole Self to God

WaterBrook

John Mark Comer and Practicing the Way

Contents

PART 01

Getting Started

Welcome

Welcome to the Fasting Practice. For over a thousand years, fasting was one of the central practices of the Way of Jesus. Apprentices of Jesus typically fasted twice a week until sundown—on Wednesdays and Fridays, as well as the 40 days of Lent. Not unlike the reading of Scripture or attending church on Sunday, fasting was simply one of the things that practicing Christians did.

After all, Jesus began his life's work with 40 days of fasting and continued to fast throughout his lifetime. And he said, "Follow me."* It makes sense that we would follow his example and incorporate fasting—in both longer and shorter intervals—into our Rule of Life, or our overall life architecture of discipleship to Jesus.

And yet, very few followers of Jesus in the modern West fast at all.

There are all sorts of reasons for this: the influence of the Enlightenment, cultural hedonism, the widespread availability of food because of modern agribusiness, the (false) advertising of the food industry telling us that we need three meals a day, the confusion of appetite with hunger (which are not the same thing), or the struggle with disordered eating and body shame. But the greatest reason is likely the West's emphasis on the mind over the body. We've lost sight of the human as a whole person—mind and body and soul. Fasting is one of the most essential and powerful of all the practices of Jesus, helping us integrate our whole bodily selves to our center in God.

But remember: The ultimate aim of fasting is to get in touch with our hunger for God. When we fast, we awaken our bodies and souls to their deep yearning for life with the Father. We become able to say with Jesus, "I have food to eat that you know nothing about."**

---

* Matthew 4v19.
** John 4v32.

The Nine Practices

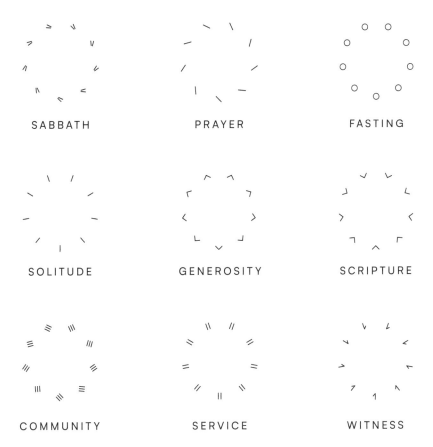

SABBATH

PRAYER

FASTING

SOLITUDE

GENEROSITY

SCRIPTURE

COMMUNITY

SERVICE

WITNESS

Fasting is just one of nine core Practices in the body of resources available from Practicing the Way. The Practices are spiritual disciplines centered around the life rhythms of Jesus. They are designed not to add even more to your already overbusy life, but to slow you down and create space for the Spirit of God to form you to be with Jesus, become like him, and do what he did. Ultimately, they are a way to experience the love of God.

To run another Practice or learn more, turn to page 92.

How to Use This Guide

A few things you need to know

This Practice is designed to be done in community, whether with a few friends around a table, within your small group, in a larger class format, or with your entire church.

The Practice is four sessions long. We recommend meeting together every week or every other week. For those of you who want to spend more time on this Practice, we've included an additional four weeks of material in the appendix to go deeper in Scripture and discussion. You are welcome to pause for these bonus conversations in between sessions or skip over them.

You will all need a copy of this Companion Guide. You can purchase a print or ebook version from your preferred book retailer. We recommend the print version so you can stay away from your devices during the Practices, as well as take notes during each session. But we realize that digital works better for some.

Each session should take about one to two hours, depending on how long you set aside for discussion and whether or not you begin with a meal. See the sample session on the following page.

Are you a group leader or facilitator? See page 96 for helpful information and additional ideas and tips on running this Practice.

Our Practices are designed to work in a variety of group sizes and environments. For that reason, your gatherings may include additional elements like meals or worship time, or may follow a structure slightly different from the following sample. Please adapt as you see fit.

Sample Session

Here is what a typical session could look like.

Welcome
Welcome the group and open in prayer.

Introduction (2–3 min.)
Watch the introduction and pause the video when indicated for your first discussion.

Discussion 01: Practice reflection in triads (15–20 min.)
Process your previous week's spiritual exercise in smaller groups of three to five people with the questions in the Guide.

Teaching (20 min.)
Watch the teaching portion of the video.

Discussion 02: Group conversation (15–30 min.)
Pause the video when indicated for a group-wide conversation.

Testimony and tutorial (5–10 min.)
Watch the rest of the video.

Prayer to close
Close by praying the liturgy in the Guide, or however you choose.

The Weekly Rhythm

The four sessions of this Practice are designed to follow a four-part rhythm that is based on our model of spiritual formation.

IN COMMUNITY

Learn
about the Way of Jesus.

Practice
with spiritual exercises using your Companion Guide.

WEEKLY RHYTHM

Process together
what is coming up for you through your experience.

Reflect
on your experience with God.

ON YOUR OWN

01 Learn

Gather together as a community for an interactive experience of learning about the Way of Jesus through teaching, storytelling, and discussion. Bring your Guide to the session and follow along.

02 Practice

On your own, before the next session, go and "put it into practice,"* as Jesus himself said. We will provide weekly spiritual disciplines and spiritual exercises, as well as recommended resources to go deeper.

03 Reflect

Reflection is key to spiritual formation. After your practice and before the next session, set aside 10–15 minutes to reflect on your experience. Reflection questions are included in this Guide at the end of each session.

04 Process together

When you come back together, begin by sharing your reflections with your group. This moment is crucial because we need each other to process our lives before God and make sense of our stories. If you are meeting in a larger group, you will need to break into smaller subgroups for this conversation so everyone has a chance to share.

---

* Philippians 4v9.

Tips on Beginning a New Practice

This Guide is full of spiritual exercises, time-tested strategies, and good advice on the spiritual discipline of fasting.

But it's important to note that the Practices are not formulaic. We can't use them to control our spiritual formation or even our relationship with God. Sometimes they don't even work very well.

The key with the spiritual disciplines is to let go of outcomes and just offer them up to Jesus in love.

Because it's so easy to lose sight of the ultimate aim of a Practice, here are a few tips to keep in mind as you practice fasting.

01 Start small

Start where you are, not where you "should" be. It's counterintuitive, but the smaller the start, the better chance you have of really sticking to it and growing over time.

02 Think subtraction, not addition

Don't try to add fasting into your already overbusy, overfull life. You are likely already overwhelmed. Instead, think: Formation is about less, not more. About slowing down and simplifying your life around what matters most: life with Jesus.

03 You get out what you put in

The more fully you give yourself to this Practice, the more life-changing it will be; the more you just dabble in it, the more shortcuts you take, the less of an effect it will have on your transformation. It's up to you: We make invitations, you make decisions.

04 Remember the J curve

Experts on learning tell us that whenever we set out to master a new skill, it tends to follow a J-shaped curve; we tend to get worse before we get better. That's okay. Expect it to be a bit difficult at first; it will get easier in time. Just stay with the Practice.

05 There is no formation without repetition

Spiritual formation is slow, deep, cumulative work that happens over years, not weeks. The goal of this four-week experience is just to get you started on a journey of a lifetime. Upon completion of this Practice, you will have a map for the journey ahead, and hopefully some possible companions for the Way.

But what you do next is up to you.

We are aware that some people may have medical issues or concerns that keep them from fasting. If this is you, please check in with a doctor or therapist before participating in this Practice. As a community, ask how you can support and include those who need to modify this Practice.

Before You Begin

The following resources are designed to enhance your experience of the Fasting Practice, but they are entirely optional.

Recommended reading

Reading a book alongside the Fasting Practice can greatly enhance your understanding and enjoyment of this discipline. You may love to read, or you may not. For that reason, it's recommended, but certainly not required.

The recommended reading for the Fasting Practice is *God's Chosen Fast* by Arthur Wallis.

Arthur Wallis (1922–1988) was a British Bible teacher who wrote this beloved book in 1968. (While there are some antiquated examples and language, it's a beautiful guide for fasting to this day.)

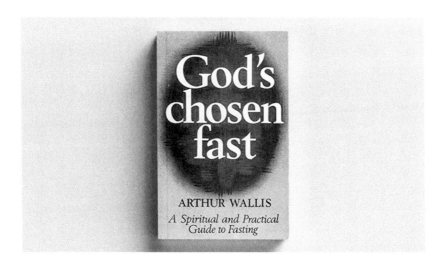

The Spiritual Health Reflection

One final note: Before you begin Session 01, please set aside 20–30 minutes and take the Spiritual Health Reflection. This is a self-assessment we developed in partnership with pastors and leading experts in spiritual formation. It's designed to help you reflect on the health of your soul in order to better name Jesus' invitations to you as you follow the Way.

You can come back to the Spiritual Health Reflection as often as you'd like (we recommend one to two times a year) to chart your growth and continue to move forward on your spiritual journey.

To access the Spiritual Health Reflection, visit practicingtheway.org/reflection and create an account. Answer the prompt questions slowly and prayerfully.

The Practicing the Way Primer

If this is your first time engaging with a Practicing the Way resource, we invite you to set aside 15 minutes before Session 01 to watch a primer on spiritual formation. This will give you a brief overview of the "why" behind spiritual practices and key insights to guard and guide your coming practice.

Log in to your online Dashboard or sign up to watch the primer at launch.practicingtheway.org.

PART 02

The Sessions

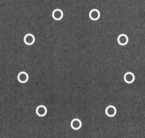

To Offer Ourselves to Jesus

Overview

In the modern world, you are more likely to hear about fasting from a Muslim, Buddhist, nutrition expert, or fitness guru than from a serious disciple of Jesus. Most followers of Jesus in the West no longer fast; if they do, it's rarely on a weekly basis, despite the fact that it was the common practice of the Church for well over a millennium and a half.

Yet in his teaching on fasting in Matthew 6v16, Jesus said, "When you fast . . ." Not "If you fast. . . ." He assumed his apprentices would follow his example by fasting.

What if we are missing out on one of the most essential and powerful of all the practices of Jesus?

One of the reasons fasting has fallen by the wayside in the Western church is that we have lost sight of what Pope John Paul II called a "theology of the body." In the biblical view, you don't have a body; you are a body. Your body is a part of who you are as a human.

This means that we can't simply think our way into spiritual maturity. Our discipleship to Jesus must take seriously our bodies, as they are "temples of the Holy Spirit"*—where we make room for God to dwell.

Most of us are used to approaching our spiritual formation and life with God through the mind—by thinking, talking, praying, reading, or hearing teaching and preaching. But few of us are comfortable approaching our spiritual formation through our stomachs, or our bodies as a whole.

Fasting is one of the best disciplines we have to reintegrate our minds to our bodies and offer our whole selves to God in surrender.

_____

* 1 Corinthians 6v19.

Opening Questions

When instructed, circle up in triads (smaller groups of three to five people) and discuss the following questions:

01 Is fasting a new practice for you in your discipleship? What experience do you have with it so far?

02 What fears or questions do you have as you begin to practice fasting?

03 What would you love to see God do in your life or your community through this practice?

Teaching

Key Scripture

When you fast, do not look somber as the hypocrites do, for they disfigure their faces to show others they are fasting. Truly I tell you, they have received their reward in full. But when you fast, put oil on your head and wash your face, so that it will not be obvious to others that you are fasting, but only to your Father, who is unseen; and your Father, who sees what is done in secret, will reward you.

—Matthew 6v16–18

Session summary

- For millennia, God's people have regularly abstained from food as a spiritual discipline.

- The definition of fasting is "not eating food." While abstinence from other habits (social media, alcohol, etc.) can be helpful, it's different from the practice of fasting.

- Fasting allows us to yearn for God with our whole selves—getting our discipleship into our hungry bodies.

- Jesus doesn't give specific requirements for fasting. But historically (and across the globe), the Church has fasted for two days out of every week, as well as calling for targeted fasts in times of crisis.

Teaching Notes

As you watch Session 01 together, feel free to use this page to take notes.

Discussion Questions

Now it's time for a conversation about the teaching. Pause the video for a few minutes to discuss in small groups:

01 What did you just learn that was new or provocative to you?

02 What do you expect your greatest challenge will be as you practice fasting?

03 If you could put into one word what you most desire from this practice, what would that word be? And why?

Practice Notes

As you continue to watch Session 01 together, feel free to use this page to take notes.

Closing Prayer

End your time together by praying this liturgy:

Father, you have made our bodies holy;
they are who we are, and they are good.
Help us to draw them into prayer,
into your presence, into holy becoming,
that we may know and love you more.

Exercise

Fast for one day this week, focusing on offering yourself to Jesus.

For the Fasting Practice, each week's exercise will be similar and straightforward: fast for one full day until sundown. Each week, we will attempt to focus our hearts on the reason for fasting we covered in that week's session. This week, focus on reason one: offering ourselves to Jesus.

A few basic tips

01   Drink tons of water to stay hydrated (unless you choose to do a total fast, no food or water).

02   If you normally drink coffee to wake up, you may want to still have coffee to avoid a caffeine headache, but just have it black. Coffee is 99.9 percent water and will not keep your body from entering the fasting state.

03   The more time you can give to prayer and reflection, and the less busy you are that day, the better. Make it your goal to slow down the day you fast and be present to your body, and God, as much as you possibly can. You may want to find a park on your lunch break or take a few short walks throughout your day. Give as much attention to God as is doable.

Resist the urge to judge your experience. Release thoughts like, I liked it; I disliked it. I felt close to God; I didn't feel close to God. *Just let the experience of fasting be what it is, and offer it to God in love.*

- Pick a day that works for you. Wednesdays or Fridays are ideal if you want to get in touch with Christians around the world and throughout church history.

- If possible, pick a day to do this together as a community; this will help to encourage and enliven your weekly practice.

- Fast until sundown that day, then eat a simple meal in gratitude.

- If a full day is too much for your body or soul, start smaller. Skip breakfast and break the fast at lunch or 3 pm. Remember: The goal is to make fasting a part of your regular life, not try it once or twice, hate it, and never try it again. Start where you are, not where you feel like you should be.

- In the time you'd normally be grocery shopping, cooking, eating, or cleaning, give yourself to prayer. Let your desire for food point you to Jesus as you open yourself to him.

- In your dedicated times of prayer, or each time a hunger pang comes, you may want to pray Romans 12v1–2, or simply, "God, I offer my body to you in worship. Please transform me."

- As you go about your day—your morning commute, caregiving, email, errands—just enjoy God's company and attempt to open your heart to him all through the day.

- If you've never fasted before, you may feel "hangry" or tired. Keep in mind that these symptoms will go away in time if you stick with the practice. You'll start to feel better, not worse.

Reach Exercise

We recognize that we're all at different stages of discipleship and seasons of life. To that end, we've added a Reach Exercise to each of the four sessions for those who have the time, energy, and desire to go further in fasting.

Fast for two days, like the early Christians.

- You may want to adopt the Wednesday and Friday rhythm like they did, or pick different days that work better for your schedule.

- Just avoid fasting on the Sabbath or the Lord's Day, as Sunday is for feasting, not fasting.

Practice Reflection

Reflection is a key component in our spiritual formation.

Millennia ago, King David prayed in Psalm 139v23–24:
> Search me, God, and know my heart;
>> test me and know my anxious thoughts.

> See if there is any offensive way in me,
>> and lead me in the way everlasting.

South African professor Trevor Hudson has quoted one of his pastoral supervisors as saying, "We do not learn from experience; we learn from reflection upon experience."* If you want to get the most out of this Practice, you need to do it and then reflect on it.

---

* Trevor Hudson, *A Mile in My Shoes: Cultivating Compassion* (Nashville, Tenn.: Upper Room Books, 2005), 57.

> Before your next time together with the group for the next session, take five to ten minutes to journal your answers to the following three questions:

01 Where did I feel resistance?

02 Where did I feel joy?

03 Where did I most experience God's nearness?

Note: As you write, be as specific as possible. While bullet points are fine, if you write it out in narrative form, your brain will be able to process your insights in a more lasting way.

Reflection Notes

Keep Growing (Optional)

The following resources were created to enhance your experience of this Practice, but they are entirely optional.

📖 Read

God's Chosen Fast by Arthur Wallis
Chapters 01–05

ılılı Listen

Rule of Life podcast on fasting
Episode 01

💬 Bonus Conversation

If you would like to slow down this four-week Practice to give your community more time to sit in each week's teaching and spiritual exercise, you can pause and meet for an optional bonus conversation in the appendix.

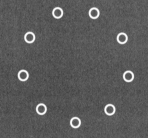

To Grow in Holiness

Overview

St. Augustine of Hippo, when asked, "Why fast?" said, "Because it is sometimes necessary to check the delight of the flesh in respect to licit pleasures in order to keep it from yielding to illicit joys."*

Like most ancient Christian intellectuals, he saw gluttony as the first of the seven deadly sins, and saw a Christian's relationship to food as a key part of their relationship to God. Most of us can see this link by direct experience: An inability to control one's appetite has a ripple effect across the whole person, often resulting in a corresponding inability to control other bodily appetites—for drink, sex, speech, gossip, consumerism, power, and dominion over others.

But on the flip side, many luminaries from the Way of Jesus have considered fasting to be a way to feed your spirit and starve your flesh, the part of our person that is bent toward sin.

Fasting does at least four things to our bodies and souls.

01   It's weaning us off the pleasure principle.

02   It's revealing what's in our heart.

03   It's reordering our desires.

04   It's drawing on the power of God to overcome sin.

Our fight is not *against* the body—the body is broken, but it's a good gift. Our fight is for the body. It's against the flesh, or sinful appetites within us all. And fasting is one of the most powerful disciplines of the Way to free our bodies and souls from the chains of sin and the prison of shame.

---

* Augustine, "The Usefulness of Fasting," *The Fathers of the Church* 16, trans. Mary Sarah Muldowney (New York: Fathers of the Church, 1952), 411.

Reflection Questions

When instructed, circle up in triads (smaller groups of three to five people) and discuss the following questions:

01   What was your experience like?

02   Where did you feel resistance?

03   Where did you feel delight?

Teaching

Key Scripture

For I do not understand my own actions. For I do not do what I want, but I do the very thing I hate. Now if I do what I do not want, I agree with the law, that it is good. So now it is no longer I who do it, but sin that dwells within me. For I know that nothing good dwells in me, that is, in my flesh. For I have the desire to do what is right, but not the ability to carry it out. For I do not do the good I want, but the evil I do not want is what I keep on doing. Now if I do what I do not want, it is no longer I who do it, but sin that dwells within me.

So I find it to be a law that when I want to do right, evil lies close at hand. For I delight in the law of God, in my inner being, but I see in my members another law waging war against the law of my mind and making me captive to the law of sin that dwells in my members. Wretched man that I am! Who will deliver me from this body of death?

—Romans 7v15–24 (ESV)

Session summary

- The spiritual discipline of fasting is not only good for physical health; it's an avenue to grow in holiness.

- Fasting helps us dedicate our whole selves—soul and body—to God.

- As Paul tells us, our sinful appetites trap us in cycles of frustration and despair.

- We can't conquer these appetites with willpower, but through the Holy Spirit, fasting can transform our desires.

- And as we put our flesh to death, God raises us up to the beautiful union with him that we were made for.

Teaching Notes

As you watch Session 02 together, feel free to use this page to take notes.

Discussion Questions

Now it's time for a conversation about the teaching. Pause the video for a few minutes to discuss in small groups:

01   What idea stuck out to you from the teaching?

02   What do you think about the idea of using your body to change your heart toward God and sin?

03   How can we, as a community, be there for one another in our struggle against sin and for holiness?

Practice Notes

As you continue to watch Session 02 together, feel free to use this page to take notes.

Closing Prayer

End your time together by praying this liturgy:

Teach us, Lord, to give up every lesser-than pleasure in the pursuit of giving ourselves wholly to you. That in giving up what we think we want, we may receive that which we truly do want—you.

Exercise

Fast for one day this week, focusing on growing in holiness.

- Pick a day that works for you. Again, Wednesdays or Fridays are ideal if you want to get in touch with Christians around the world and throughout church history.

- If possible, pick a day to do this together as a community; this will help to encourage and enliven your weekly practice.

- Fast until sundown that day, then eat a simple meal in gratitude.

- If a full day is too much for your body or soul, start smaller. Skip breakfast and break the fast at lunch or 3 pm. Each week, try to stretch your fast time a little longer. If last week was until noon, try for 2 pm this week.

- In the time you'd normally be grocery shopping, cooking, eating, or cleaning, give yourself to prayer, and focus your heart on this second motivation for fasting: to grow in holiness.

- In your dedicated times of prayer, or each time a hunger pang comes, you may want to pray, "God, purify my heart and purge my whole person of sin."

- If possible, set aside time in the quiet or in deep conversation with a close spiritual friend, and ask God to reveal any sin in your life he is targeting for freedom. Offer it to God in confession, repentance, and prayer.

Reach Exercise

This week's Reach Exercise is the same as last week's.

Fast for two days, like the early Christians.

- You may want to adopt the Wednesday and Friday rhythm like they did, or pick different days that work better for your schedule.

- But avoid fasting on the Sabbath or the Lord's Day, as Sunday is for feasting, not fasting.

Practice Reflection

Before your next time together with the group for Session 03, take five to ten minutes to journal your answers to the following three questions:

O1   What surprised me during my day of fasting?

O2   What did I notice about myself while I was hungry?

O3   Did I sense any changes in myself after my fast?

Note: As you write, be as specific as possible. While bullet points are fine, if you write it out in narrative form, your brain will be able to process your insights in a more lasting way.

Reflection Notes

Keep Growing (Optional)

The following resources were created to enhance your experience of this Practice, but they are entirely optional.

📖 Read

God's Chosen Fast by Arthur Wallis
Chapters 06–10

ᶴᶴ Listen

Rule of Life podcast on fasting
Episode 02

💬 Bonus Conversation

If you would like to slow down this four-week Practice to give your community more time to sit in each week's teaching and spiritual exercise, you can pause and meet for an optional bonus conversation in the appendix.

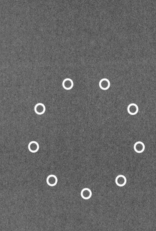

To Amplify
Our Prayers

Overview

Fasting and prayer go together. Like two wings of a bird, together they take flight. You can pray without fasting, and you can fast without praying, but when you combine the two, there's a noticeable amplification of your prayer before God. This comes as no surprise, since fasting is a kind of praying with our bodies. When the requests of our hearts are coupled with the yearnings of our bodies, our prayers are purified of their dross and presented like precious metal before the Father, for him to do as he will.

Of course, "prayer" is an umbrella term for the medium through which we communicate and commune with God. Prayer involves both speaking and listening. And fasting is a key companion in both.

Fasting is an aid in *hearing* God.

It helps us to discern his voice through the noise and distraction of our lives. It sharpens our minds; in the fasting state, our minds are more alert, focused, and open. It makes it easier for us to hear how God is coming to us, to hear his will, and to hear his direction for our lives.

But fasting is also an aid to *being heard* by God.

It helps us to break through the walls that stand between us and the release of God's plans, purposes, and power. Story after story—in Scripture and church history—attest to this reality: When prayer and fasting link arms, it's often the tipping point in the struggle to release God's Kingdom, on earth as it is in heaven.

Reflection Questions

When instructed, circle up in triads (smaller groups of three to five people) and discuss the following questions:

01 Did you notice any shift in your heart toward sin while you were fasting?

02 What's an area in your life where your willpower is failing and you are praying for the grace to change?

03 What's an area in your life where you are experiencing increasing freedom from sin and joy in God?

Teaching

Key Scripture

Now in the church at Antioch there were prophets and teachers: Barnabas, Simeon called Niger, Lucius of Cyrene, Manaen (who had been brought up with Herod the tetrarch) and Saul. While they were worshiping the Lord and fasting, the Holy Spirit said, "Set apart for me Barnabas and Saul for the work to which I have called them." So after they had fasted and prayed, they placed their hands on them and sent them off.

—Acts 13v1–3

Session summary

- Over time, fasting becomes a calming and clarifying process, creating ideal conditions for hearing God's voice.

- Fasting is a key aid in helping us discern God's will for our lives, particularly when we're facing major decisions.

- Fasting powerfully amplifies our prayers, bringing our bodies into conversation with God.

- While God's ways are mysterious, Scripture is clear that God responds to prayer and fasting.

- Fasting isn't about getting what we want from God, but bringing us into loving communion with him.

Teaching Notes

As you watch Session 03 together, feel free to use this page to take notes.

Discussion Questions

Now it's time for a conversation about the teaching. Pause the video for a few minutes to discuss in small groups:

01 Do you have any stories of clear answers to prayer?

02 What's an area in your current life where you are praying for discernment, seeking to know the will of God for your life direction?

03 What's an area in your current life where you are praying for a breakthrough?

Practice Notes

As you continue to watch Session 03 together, feel free to use this page to take notes.

Closing Prayer

End your time together by praying this liturgy:

Empower us, Holy Spirit, and
all our prayers, as we offer
our bodies in harmony with
our deepest yearnings.
We need your in-breaking power,
your grace, your listening,
that your Kingdom and will
may be done amidst us now
and forever.

Exercise

Fast for one day this week, focusing on how it amplifies your prayers.

- Pick a day that works for you; we recommend Wednesdays or Fridays.

- If possible, pick a day that works for your community to fast together.

- Fast until sundown that day, then eat a simple meal in gratitude.

- In the time you'd normally be grocery shopping, cooking, eating, or cleaning, give yourself to prayer.

- In your dedicated times of prayer, or each time a hunger pang comes, you may want to pray through a short list of specific requests you are holding before God, or simply pray, "God, speak to me. I'm listening."

- If possible, set aside time in the quiet to listen for God's voice and offer your prayers up to God. You may want to get up early, find a quiet park on your lunch break, or end your day with a nice walk. But find a time and place to minimize distractions and combine your fasting with prayer.

Reach Exercise

Fast for a longer period of time.

- If you have the desire and life space to increase the duration of your fasting practice, this could be an ideal week to do a longer fast.

- You may want to fast for a full day, eating dinner one night and not breaking the fast until the morning 36 hours later.

- Or you may feel invited by the Spirit of Jesus into a multi-day fast of two days, three days, or longer.

- Just remember: Unless there is a clear stirring in your heart from the Spirit to pursue a longer fast, the best practice is to "walk before you run." If you've only ever fasted until sundown, try just going until the following morning as your next step in the journey.

Practice Reflection

Before your next time together with the group for Session 04, take five to ten minutes to journal your answers to the following three questions:

01 How did it feel to pray while being hungry?

02 Have I sensed any direction from God's Spirit?

03 What am I longing for God to do with my heart, soul, mind, and body?

Note: As you write, be as specific as possible. While bullet points are fine, if you write it out in narrative form, your brain will be able to process your insights in a more lasting way.

Reflection Notes

Keep Growing (Optional)

The following resources were created to enhance your experience of this Practice, but they are entirely optional.

📖 Read

God's Chosen Fast by Arthur Wallis
Chapters 11–15

ᐧ�|I|ᐧ Listen

Rule of Life podcast on fasting
Episode 03

💬 Bonus Conversation

If you would like to slow down this four-week Practice to give your community more time to sit in each week's teaching and spiritual exercise, you can pause and meet for an optional bonus conversation in the appendix.

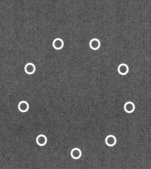

To Stand with the Poor

Overview

Give to the hungry what you deny your own appetite.

—Saint Gregory of Nyssa

In the West, many of us struggle with the problem of food abundance—having too much food to eat. Our pantries overflow with snacks; we have so much food in our fridges it goes bad before we have a chance to eat it; apps like DoorDash put any food we want just a few swipes away. Dieting is a constant fad, and most of us live in a daily war of attrition against sugar, processed carbs, and over-indulgence. But most of the world, and many more people than we realize in our own neighborhoods and cities, live with food scarcity—not having enough to eat. Often, they are hiding in plain sight in our own churches and communities.

Fasting is a way to bridge this gap between "the haves" and "the have-nots." Going back at least as far as Isaiah 58, it has long been a vehicle for biblical justice, a way for those with too much food to share with those in need of food.

Early on in the history of the Church, fasting was tied to what Jesus and the early Christians called "almsgiving"—a practice that combined generosity, serving, and justice. On fasting days, Christians would take the food or money they would have spent on food and give it to the poor. Often, they would also give the time they would have spent cooking, eating, and cleaning up to serving the poor.

This simple practice of giving away the money we would have spent on ourselves has the potential to transform not only the lives of the poor, but our own lives and communities as well.

Reflection Questions

When instructed, circle up in triads (smaller groups of three to five people) and discuss the following questions:

01 Did you sense God's voice this last week in any way?

02 What's one thing you were specifically praying for?

03 How are you feeling three weeks into this new practice?

Teaching

Key Scripture

Is this the kind of fast I have chosen,
    only a day for people to humble themselves?
Is it only for bowing one's head like a reed
    and for lying in sackcloth and ashes?
Is that what you call a fast,
    a day acceptable to the LORD?

Is not this the kind of fasting I have chosen:
to loose the chains of injustice
    and untie the cords of the yoke,
to set the oppressed free
    and break every yoke?

Is it not to share your food with the hungry
    and to provide the poor wanderer with shelter—
when you see the naked, to clothe them,
    and not to turn away from your own flesh and blood?

—Isaiah 58v5–7

Session summary

- Isaiah makes it clear that God's goal for fasting includes care for those in need. It's a way to love God and love our neighbor at the same time.

- When we fast, we:
    - Stand in solidarity with the hungry.

    - Share what we have.

    - Stand against evil and injustice.

- Fasting defies the principalities and powers that create injustice in our world.

- In fasting, the Church is transformed into the family that it's meant to be.

- Rhythms of fasting and feasting point us to the coming feast in the eternal Kingdom of God.

Teaching Notes

As you watch Session 04 together, feel free to use this page to take notes.

Discussion Questions

Now it's time for a conversation about the teaching. Pause the video for a few minutes to discuss in small groups:

01 What effect do you see this practice having on you—on both your body and your soul?

02 Are you thinking of continuing this practice? If so, in what way?

03 Do we know of any practical needs that we could meet together as a community?

Practice Notes

As you continue to watch Session 04 together, feel free to use this page to take notes.

Closing Prayer

End your time together by praying this liturgy:

Help us take the overflow of
all we have, Lord, and offer
it to the lack in our world,
that in our giving up,
and our giving away,
we may show the world
what we've come to know—
your extravagant, self-offering,
and sacrificial love.

Exercise

Fast for one day this week, giving what you would have spent on food to the poor.

Our exercise for Session 04 is very similar to the previous three weeks, with one simple addition: generosity and service to the poor.

- Pick a day that works for you; we recommend Wednesdays or Fridays.

- If possible, pick a day that works for your community to fast together.

- Fast until sundown that day, then eat a simple meal in gratitude.

- In the time you'd normally be grocery shopping, cooking, eating, or cleaning, focus your heart on standing with the poor or hungry.

- Calculate the money you would have spent on breakfast and lunch and share it with the poor.

Here are a few ideas of how to do this:

- Donate the money or food to your local food bank or your church's food pantry.

- Donate the funds to a local nonprofit.

- Buy groceries for someone.

- Share your money with someone who needs help paying a medical bill or unexpected expense.

- Find a need and meet it that day.

- Pray and ask God to infuse your imagination and desire with his imagination and desire. Do whatever comes to the surface of your heart.

- As you fast, give, and serve, quietly ask God to set your heart free of self-love and self-preservation and transform you into a person of Christlike *agape*.

Reach Exercise

Serve the poor.

- Our final Reach Exercise is to not only share your food money with the poor, but to find a place to serve those in need in your community or city; to make a relational move toward the poor, treating them not as objects of pity, but as brothers and sisters.

- You may want to serve with a local nonprofit or volunteer for a justice initiative with your church, or simply find someone you know with a practical need. The more relational, the better.

- The end goal isn't just to share with the poor, or even to serve the poor, but to become family with the poor. As you do, you will see the face of Jesus in often unexpected places.

Practice Reflection

Take five to ten minutes to journal your answers to the following three questions:

01   Did I notice any need in my community this week?

02   How did my heart react to this week's focus on justice?

03   Have I sensed any changes in myself during this Practice?

Note: As you write, be as specific as possible. While bullet points are fine, if you write it out in narrative form, your brain will be able to process your insights in a more lasting way.

Reflection Notes

Keep Growing (Optional)

The following resources were created to enhance your experience of this Practice, but they are entirely optional.

📖 Read

God's Chosen Fast by Arthur Wallis
Chapters 16–20

ᯤ Listen

Rule of Life podcast on fasting
Episode 04

💬 Bonus Conversation

If you would like to slow down this four-week Practice to give your community more time to sit in each week's teaching and spiritual exercise, you can pause and meet for an optional bonus conversation in the appendix.

May God himself,
the God of peace,
sanctify you through and through.
May your whole spirit, soul and body
be kept blameless at the coming of our Lord Jesus Christ.

—1 Thessalonians 5v23

PART 03

Continue the Journey

What's Next?

You are not going to explore the full scope of the ancient practice of fasting in four weeks. This short Practice is only designed to get you moving on a lifelong journey. The weekly fasting rhythm you've been practicing is meant to be integrated into your Rule of Life, should you so choose. You may choose to make fasting a rhythmic part of your discipleship, on a weekly or monthly basis, or you may want to practice responsive fasting, regularly responding to life's sacred events with all you've learned through this Practice.

Further Practice

Where you go from here is entirely up to you, but if you decide to integrate fasting into your life, here's a list of next steps to continue your practice.

01 Go on a solitude retreat

- Jesus went into the wilderness, practicing silence, solitude, fasting, and Scripture. His "retreat" was 40 days long; yours can be much shorter. Start with an overnight. But you can emulate Jesus' foray into the wilderness by practicing fasting while in solitude and silence and immersing yourself in Scripture.

- This would be an especially good idea if you're in a season of discernment and facing a major decision where you really desire to hear God's voice of direction.

02 Fast for a longer period of time

- There's no "right" length, as fasting is never once commanded by Jesus or required by the New Testament writers. But many have found that a onetime or infrequent longer fast (of a week or 21 days) can be a before/after moment in one's spiritual journey.

- The key is to only do this if you sense the Spirit's invitation. Do not practice this out of idealism, spiritual heroism, or a misplaced desire for weight loss or a spiritual high.

03 Call your church or community to a fast

- You can organize a fast for a larger group of people around a specific aim, such as revival in your church or city.

- It's best to meet daily during community-wide fasts, for prayer and mutual encouragement.

Recommended Reading

Here are some of our favorite books on fasting as a spiritual discipline, for those of you who desire to learn more:

Fasting
by Scot McKnight

New Testament theologian Scot McKnight places the practice of fasting within a theology of the whole body.

The Spirituality of Fasting
by Charles M. Murphy

Catholic priest Charles Murphy walks through fasting as a pillar of Christian faith in this short, reader-friendly book.

How to Fast
by Reward Sibanda

Pastor Reward Sibanda explains how biblical fasting leads to deeper communion with God.

Eat, Fast, Feast
by Jay W. Richards

American philosopher Jay Richards combines the spiritual history of fasting with recent research on its health effects.

The Practices

Information alone isn't enough to produce transformation.

By adopting not just the teaching but also the practices from Jesus' own life, we open up our entire beings to God and allow him to transform us into people of love.

Our nine core Practices work together to form a Rule of Life for the modern era.

Sabbath	**Prayer**	**Fasting**
Solitude	**Generosity**	**Scripture**
Community	**Service**	**Witness**

WHAT'S INCLUDED FOR EACH PRACTICE

Four Sessions
Each session includes teaching, guided discussion, and weekly exercises to integrate the Practices into daily life.

Companion Guide
A detailed guide provides question prompts, session-by-session exercises, and space to write and reflect.

Recommended Resources
Additional recommended readings and podcasts offer a way to get the most out of the Practices.

Learn more by visiting practicingtheway.org/resources.

The Practicing the Way Course

An eight-session primer on spiritual formation.

Two thousand years ago, Jesus said to his disciples, "Follow me." But what does it mean for us to follow Jesus today?

The Practicing the Way Course is an on-ramp to spiritual formation, exploring what it means to follow Jesus and laying the foundation for a life of apprenticeship to him.

WHAT'S INCLUDED

Eight Sessions
John Mark and other voices teaching on apprenticing under Jesus, spiritual formation, healing from sin, meeting God in pain, crafting a Rule of Life, living in community, and more

Exercises
Weekly practices and exercises to help integrate what you've learned into your everyday life

Guided Conversation
Prompts to reflect on your experience and process honestly in community

Companion Guide
A detailed workbook with exercises, space to write and reflect, and suggestions for supplemental resources

Learn more by visiting practicingtheway.org/resources.

Practicing the Way:
Be with him. Become like him. Do as he did.

The first followers of Jesus developed a Rule of Life, or habits and practices based on the life of Jesus himself. As they learned to live like their teacher, they became people who made space for God to do his most transformative work in their lives.

Practicing the Way is a vision for the future, shaped by the wisdom of the past. It's an introduction to spiritual formation accessible to both beginners and lifelong followers of Jesus and a companion to the Practicing the Way Course (practicingtheway.org/course). This book offers theological substance, astute cultural insight, and practical wisdom for creating a Rule of Life (practicingtheway.org/ruleoflifebuilder) in the modern age.

You can order your copy or get copies for your community at practicingtheway.org/book or through your preferred bookseller.

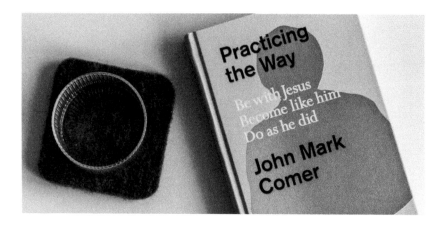

The Fasting Practice

The Circle

Practicing the Way is a nonprofit that develops spiritual formation resources for churches and small groups learning how to become apprentices in the Way of Jesus.

We believe one of the greatest needs of our time is for people to discover how to become lifelong disciples of Jesus. To that end, we help people learn how to be with Jesus, become like him, and do as he did, through the practices and rhythms he and his earliest followers lived by.

All of our downloadable ministry resources are available at no cost, thanks to the generosity of The Circle and other givers from around the world who partner with us to see formation integrated into the Church at large.

To learn more or join us, visit practicingtheway.org/give.

For Facilitators

Before you begin, there are three easy things you need to do (this should only take 10–15 minutes).

01   Go to launch.practicingtheway.org, log in, create a group, and send a digital invitation to your community. This will give your group access to the Spiritual Health Reflection, videos, and all sorts of valuable extras. Encourage your group to bring along their Companion Guide to each session, as it contains the discussion questions and space to take notes.

> ○ You can purchase a print or ebook version from your preferred book retailer. We recommend the print version so you can stay away from your devices during the Practices, as well as take notes during each session. But we realize that digital works better for some.

> ○ Note: You can order the Guides ahead of time and have them waiting when people arrive for Session 01, or encourage people to order or download their own and bring them to your gatherings.

02   Send a message to your group encouraging everyone to take the Spiritual Health Reflection before your first gathering. You can direct your group to practicingtheway.org/reflection.

03   If your group has not been through the Practicing the Way Course, invite them to watch the short primer in the online Dashboard before you gather for Session 01 of this Practice.

For training, tips, and more resources for facilitating the Fasting Practice, log in to the Dashboard at launch.practicingtheway.org.

APPENDIX

Bonus Conversations

To Offer Ourselves to Jesus

Read this introduction and Scripture together before discussing.

Paul's call in Romans 12 is simple yet radical: Give your whole self—body, mind, and soul—to God as a living act of worship. But this isn't just about behavior; it's a whole new way of being in the world. It's about resisting the quiet but constant pull of culture, which tries to mold us in its image, and instead letting God's Spirit renew our minds so we start to see, feel, and respond to the world as Jesus would. With this renewed way of thinking, we'll begin to sense what God's will really is—a life aligned with everything he calls good, beautiful, and whole.

Now, let's talk about how these principles relate to fasting. In a world obsessed with excess, what does it look like for our minds to be renewed as we offer our bodies to God through hunger?

Therefore, I urge you, brothers and sisters, in view of God's mercy, to offer your bodies as a living sacrifice, holy and pleasing to God—this is your true and proper worship. Do not conform to the pattern of this world, but be transformed by the renewing of your mind. Then you will be able to test and approve what God's will is—his good, pleasing and perfect will.

—Romans 12v1–2

Discuss the Scripture

01   What do you notice as you read this passage from Romans 12? What stands out to you, and why?

02   Consider the phrase "in view of God's mercy." Can you remember a specific moment when you encountered God's mercy in a way that changed you? What did that experience do to your heart, your mind, or your body?

03   What would it practically look like for you to "offer your [body] as a living sacrifice"? How does this relate to fasting in your life—what might God be inviting you into through this act?

04   Romans 12v1–2 invites us to reflect on the connection between our minds and bodies. Consider one specific habit you engage in regularly—whether it's good or bad. What thoughts or beliefs are at the root of that habit? What new thoughts or perspectives can be renewed in you so that this habit becomes an intentional act of worship to God?

Discuss the practice

01   How do you approach fasting right now? Is it something you've embraced or maybe avoided?

02   As you prepare to fast this week, how can you start inviting Jesus into the moments of desire or hunger that will inevitably arise—even before you begin?

03   What emotions do you anticipate feeling while fasting? Are there specific feelings you're bracing for or maybe hoping for?

04   The world sees fasting in all sorts of ways—often disconnected from its full purpose. How do you think God wants to renew our minds to perceive it more accurately?

To Grow in Holiness

Our culture often overlooks it, but fasting is a powerful way to repent and return our hearts, minds, and bodies to an honest relationship with God. It's not about fasting to stay in shape or ticking off a religious box. God isn't interested in empty rituals. He desires a genuine, authentic relationship with his people and wants our hearts.

"Even now," declares the LORD, "return
to me with all your heart, with
fasting and weeping and mourning."

Rend your heart
　　and not your garments.
Return to the LORD your God,
　　for he is gracious and compassionate,
slow to anger and abounding in love,
　　and he relents from sending calamity.

—Joel 2v12–13

Discuss the Scripture

01 As you sit with this passage, what catches your attention? Is there a word, phrase, or idea that seems to linger?

02 Is there an area of sin or struggle in your life that you have avoided addressing? How could fasting help you face this head-on?

03 We can't simply will ourselves to weep and mourn. What might we need to understand about our own sin—and the brokenness around us—to honestly grieve and turn our hearts back to God?

04 How does the writer describe God's character here? How does knowing these traits shape the way you come to him in moments of repentance?

Discuss the practice

01 How do you think fasting changes the way we see our need for God's grace in moments of failure or regret?

02 How does fasting as an act of repentance challenge our ideas of self-sufficiency and push us toward deeper dependence on God?

03 Outward practices like fasting matter when they open the door to a deeper heart shift. How do you stay present and connected to your heart during outward acts of repentance?

04 How might you embrace fasting as more than just a onetime exercise, but as an ongoing rhythm? What would it look like for fasting to shape your relationship with Jesus over time?

To Amplify Our Prayers

Read this introduction and Scripture together before discussing.

In this week's text, Queen Esther is standing on the brink of life and death, caught in a plot to annihilate her people. She faces an impossible choice: protect her position or risk her life by approaching the king uninvited, reveal her Jewish identity, and plead for the lives of her people. In this moment of desperation, she calls her people to join her in a three-day fast, seeking God's deliverance. Let's explore the role of fasting in times of crisis: how it draws us into God's purposes, sharpens our focus in confusion, and unites us in a powerful act of shared faith.

Then Esther sent this reply to Mordecai: "Go, gather together all the Jews who are in Susa, and fast for me. Do not eat or drink for three days, night or day. I and my attendants will fast as you do. When this is done, I will go to the king, even though it is against the law. And if I perish, I perish."

—Esther 4v15–16

Discuss the Scripture

01   What stands out to you as you read the passage?

02   Esther steps into a situation where the law is directly against her. What do you think this teaches us about the tension between obeying civil authorities and following God's higher law of love? How do you navigate this tension in your own life?

03   Notice that before Esther takes action, she calls for a fast. What role do you think fasting plays in preparing us for tough decisions or moments of crisis?

04   Esther says, "If I perish, I perish." What do you think this statement reveals about her? Are you willing to fast and pray, no matter what the outcome may be?

Discuss the practice

01   How does fasting in times of crisis deepen our trust in God, especially when we're unsure of the outcome?

02   In what ways does fasting help us set aside distractions, allowing us to focus more fully on God's guidance and help?

03   Have you ever faced a life-or-death situation? What situations can you imagine in your life—or in your community—where a fast from food and water might be a crucial move?

04   What role does community play in the fasting process, and how can fasting together strengthen our hope in God's ability to intervene during times of collective crisis?

To Stand with the Poor

Read this introduction and Scripture together before discussing.

Jesus, filled with the Spirit after 40 days of fasting, announces his mission: to bring good news, justice, and freedom to the poor and oppressed. Now, let's explore the connection between fasting and proclaiming justice. How does fasting align our hearts with God's desire to liberate the oppressed?

Jesus, full of the Holy Spirit, left the Jordan and was led by the Spirit into the wilderness, where for forty days he was tempted by the devil. He ate nothing during those days, and at the end of them he was hungry. . . .

Jesus returned to Galilee in the power of the Spirit, and news about him spread through the whole countryside. He was teaching in their synagogues, and everyone praised him.

He went to Nazareth, where he had been brought up, and on the Sabbath day he went into the synagogue, as was his custom. He stood up to read, and the scroll of the prophet Isaiah was handed to him. Unrolling it, he found the place where it is written:

"The Spirit of the Lord is on me,
    because he has anointed me
    to proclaim good news to the poor.
He has sent me to proclaim freedom for the prisoners
    and recovery of sight for the blind,
to set the oppressed free,
    to proclaim the year of the Lord's favor."

—Luke 4v1–2, 14–19

Discuss the Scripture

01 What catches your attention as you read through the passage?

02 Reflect on how the Holy Spirit led Jesus into the wilderness to fast and be tested. Where in your life are you leaning on the Spirit's guidance, even when it's hard?

03 Notice how Jesus' 40 days of fasting and testing preceded his proclamation of justice in quoting Isaiah 61. How might our fasting today prepare us to live out the justice and freedom that Jesus proclaimed?

04 In what ways does this passage suggest a connection between private spiritual practices and public acts of justice? What do you think happens when this connection is missing?

Discuss the practice

01 Discuss how fasting can be a form of resistance to systemic oppression. How can this practice empower us to defy the powers that perpetuate evil and injustice in our world?

02 How might fasting reveal the areas where we are complicit with systems of injustice? How could this awareness lead to real change?

03 How can fasting help us better identify with the poor and the hungry? How might this act of solidarity with the poor change your relationships with members of your city?

04 What are some other specific and tangible ways fasting frees us up to bring good news to the poor and freedom to the oppressed?